A little book about referencing and avoiding plagiarism

(very useful for international students)

Kevin Ottley

- This little book has been produced in order to help international students know how to reference in their essays, reports and other written work, and also how to avoid plagiarism.

- It has been written by someone who has twenty years' experience of teaching English as a Foreign Language, and more than ten years' experience teaching English for Academic Purposes (EAP) in universities and colleges in Britain.

- It has been written by someone who knows through experience that students who plagiarise are not wrong and are not criminals; they plagiarise because they do not understand the 'rules' about referencing and plagiarism.

What are the rules about referencing and plagiarism?

Cultural differences

You will have noticed since you started your studies in Britain, the US, Australia, Canada or New Zealand (or whatever English-speaking country you are studying in) that people do things differently in your new home: they speak differently, drive differently, use a different kind of body language; they different, have different diets and different tastes in music and fashion. Even if you are studying in your own country, you will have noticed that your English teachers – the ones who are from an English-speaking country – look, speak and act a bit differently from the way you and your friends do. In short, their culture is different from yours.

Culture is a difficult word to explain, but whatever it is, it affects every part of our lives – diet, fashion, music, language, behaviour. It also affects education. Between different cultures, people learn differently; and the process of learning has rules which are different from culture to culture. Think about driving: you will agree that in India people drive differently from in England, or that Italian and German driving habits are very different. Why is this? On the one hand, it is because the cultures of these countries are very different; but this is reflected too in the rules of driving in these places: road signs are different, as are speed limits, how much you alcohol you might be allowed to drink, seat belt regulations, headlights, etc. And education is the same: it has rules, and the rules of education are different from culture to culture.

The observation of rules

Holidaymakers and travellers often complain that the country they are visiting has rules they dislike. What they mean, usually, is that the rules are different from their own. They may wonder why this is so, they may complain about it, they may even compare these rules to their own and decide that theirs are better. But would they break the rules of the country they are visiting just because they don't like them, or because they are different? I hope not!

It is the same with the rules of education. If you are studying in, for example, Australia, you are expected to observe the rules and laws of Australian society; and if you choose to study in Australia, you are expected to study according to their rules.

Why reference?

In all cultures of learning it is important to learn facts, information, and to remember and recall these – usually during exams: examinations are, basically, a way of testing that you have learned what you should have learned. However, in some cultures of learning, this learn and recall of information is more central to education, more important, than in others. Meanwhile, there are other cultures of learning which value not learning, but originality of expression.

Most English-speaking countries follow a tradition of education where you are expected to learn facts and ideas and comment upon them, but you are not expected to have great original ideas – at least not until postgraduate level. You should never forget that you are at university to learn. If you already have your own ideas, why study at university?

You might want to think of yourself as a computer. Your aim is to 'output' data, and this you do in the form of essays, presentations, exams. But there can be no successful output without input, and reading and learning is when you input data. So you are the computer, processing the data and information which you read.

In English, there is an expression – 'to stand on the shoulders of giants' (you might know this as the motto for Google Scholar; the expression also features on the edges of British £2 coins). This expression is a wonderful description of the learning experience – you learn from the ideas of others ('giants') and then, standing on their shoulders, you can see further.

In the western educational system it is important to show where your learning comes from. This is why you reference. Basically, you cannot learn unless you read; and it is with references that you show what you have read, what you have learned. And you must do this – you do not want to make the giants angry!

It is with references that you show where your learning is from. If you do not reference, your teachers will mistakenly think that the ideas you are presenting are your own.

Referencing: it is fair!

Imagine you are invited out in the evening and you want to impress the person who is inviting you: you want to look your best! A friend,

Joe, has a black jacket which you really like and you know it looks good on you – he has already let you wear it a few times. So you ask to borrow it, and he agrees. Later in the evening the person you are meeting admires the jacket. You reply: 'thanks, but actually this belongs to my friend, Joe – he has lent it to me.' Congratulations – you have just referenced.

You have invited some friends to your apartment for dinner. You cook most of the meal yourself but add a sauce you buy from the supermarket – one produced by a company called *Matson's*. Your friends compliment you on the meal, one of them adding: 'the sauce was really nice!' You reply: 'thanks – I got the sauce from the supermarket. It's made by *Matson's*.' Congratulations – you have just referenced.

You are chatting with a friend, Sammy, about what you might do at the weekend. She suggests going to the beach. You pass on this information to others and they agree it's a wonderful idea. You reply:

'I think so too. Sammy gave me the idea.' Congratulations – you have just referenced.

The three examples above should make it clear that referencing is a fair thing to do. Read the three examples again, but imagine yourself replying: 'thanks – the jacket is mine / I invented the sauce / going to the beach is my idea.' Would that be fair? How would you feel making those false claims?

Referencing: don't upset people!

And how would Joe, *Matson's* and Sammy feel if they found out that you were claiming their ideas and inventions as your own? Not too good, I guess. For how would you feel if someone was taking your ideas and using them as their own? Would you be happy? Or angry?

Referencing: make it legal!

One of my favourite songs is Jennifer Lopez's *On the Floor* – a big hit in 2011. But if you know the song you will know it is not by Jennifer Lopez alone but includes Pitbull. In fact, the full and correct title for the song and the artist(s) is: *On the Floor* – Jennifer Lopez feat. Pitbull. 'Feat' is short for 'featuring', which comes from the verb, 'to feature'. I checked in my dictionary, and read that 'to feature' means "to include something or someone as an important part." In other words, Jennifer Lopez wants us to know that Pitbull is an important part of her song. That will make Pitbull feel better!

Including Pitbull in the song is a reference. Legally, it means that Pitbull will get some of the money which Jennifer Lopez makes from the hit. But imagine how we would feel if he helped with the song but he wasn't mentioned! Not too happy, I guess. He might even make a legal claim against Jennifer Lopez. Personally, I would not want to upset Pitbull. Not with a name like that!

Referencing and avoiding plagiarism are important academic skills

As an international student studying at an English-speaking university, you are a bit different from the home students. Together you are learning facts and information – together, you are given the same 'input'. But you are also learning language, either by being taught this in extra English classes, or by noticing words, grammar and expressions in your reading which you can later reuse. You are also learning what we call 'study skills,' how to input, process and output data most successfully – things like 'how to structure your essays,' 'how to research,' 'how to reference,' and so on. And just like you are expected to remember and recall information – data – you are also tested on your ability to use the study skills you have learned. Referencing and avoiding plagiarism are important academic skills. If you do them correctly and successfully you will pick up extra marks.

So – how do I reference?

There are two stages to referencing. First, you must refer to the source in your text. This is called a <u>citation</u>. Second, you must give full details of all the sources in the bibliography at the end of your work. This is called the <u>reference</u>. Full details of how to do both are given in this booklet.

You must reference when you

- Paraphrase (putting original ideas into your own words)
- Summarise (writing a short description of the original ideas in your own words but giving your own opinion or interpretation)
- Refer to a source (mentioning the work without giving much more information about it)
- Quote (using the actual words from the source)
- Use statistics or data

You should make and keep a careful note of everything you read when you are producing a piece of writing. If it is a book or journal, mark the book title and author. If it is a website, copy and paste the URL into a document. This way, you will always be able to find the information again later.

If you fail to reference fully and correctly, your teacher will not be clear what are your own ideas and words. Also, your teacher may think you are pretending that the words and ideas you take from sources are your own.

Definition of plagiarism. The Cambridge online dictionary (2013) defines plagiarism as "to use another person's ideas or a part of their work and pretend it is your own." This includes ideas or material from any sources. These might be written, internet or audiovisual media. It also includes work from students and academic staff.

It is surprisingly easy for your teachers to detect plagiarism. Most place of learning use sophisticated electronic software to check all student submissions. This checks against all information on the internet as well as against other student work. Your teacher will also use his/her own judgement. Remember, English is not your first language, whereas information you might include form sources is. It is not difficult, therefore, for your teacher to notice a difference in quality in your writing. Also, your teacher will have copies of work you have produced in class. If you submit a piece of writing which is suddenly much more superior in quality, your teacher will be suspicious.

Because plagiarism is wrong, universities punish students who are found guilty of plagiarism. Punishments range from having to rewrite the piece of work (usually with a cap placed on the final mark), to being summoned before an Academic Misconduct Board.

How to cite sources in your work

Inserting the author's name and date of publication

This book uses the Harvard system of referencing. This means you do not need to use any numbering or footnotes on each page. Just insert the author's name and date of publication in brackets after you summarise, paraphrase or mention the information you have taken from a source.

It is clear that house prices fell between 1992 and 1996 (Harden 2002).

When the author's name appears naturally in your work

Often, it is better to just insert the author's name, followed by the date of publication (in brackets), into your text.

According to Stanton (2011), the main difference between the two political parties is...

Paraphrasing or summarising from a specific page or pages

When you give specific information from an identifiable page or pages within a long book or report, you may want to include the page number(s) as well as the date.

Eakins (2008, p.117) argues that many readers of the paper do not understand that...

When the author is a company or organisation

Often, an organisation such as a company, a university or a government department is the author of a publication. This could also be the publisher's name. Just cite the name in the text the same as you would an author.

Research by the British Medical Association (1998) indicates that hospitals in the central region of Scotland...

When there is no author

Some publications may not include the name of a personal or even a corporate author. If this is the case, just use the publication title.

After several years of research it was discovered that the main reason children in the target age group had started smoking was pressure from children in a slightly older age group, usually from brothers and sisters (Health issues today, 2005).

When no date is available

If the source includes no date, use 'n.d.' (which means 'not dated'.) Many websites, for example, do not have a date.

All the respondents were male, in employment, and aged between 25 and 45 (Jones, n.d.).

Multiple authors

If the source has two or three authors, give their names, separated by commas and an ampersand (&) or the word 'and'. Do not forget the date of the publication.

The journal put forward several convincing arguments in favour of ending the dispute (Akram, Wiston and Earby, 2012).

If the source has four or more authors, use the name of the first author followed by either the words 'and others' or 'et al'. Make sure you continue to use this same form each time you cite from the same source.

Kleindorf and others (1984) insist that the only reliable method is...

Citing more than one author at the same point in the text

You may find that the point you are making in your work has been made by different authors in different publications. You should cite all these. List them in order of publication date (earliest first).

Kray (1996), Burns (1999) and Van Brugh (2014) all agree that the president should have consulted his prime minister before issuing the statement to the press.

You may, if you wish, use semicolons to separate the authors' names.

Most research in the area (Klee 2003; Lilly; 2004; Heward; 2008) indicates that...

When the author has more than one item published in the same year

Use lower case letters after the date to make it clear that you are citing different sources.

Anderson (2010a) gives a very strong argument in favour of...

[followed later in the assignment by]

On the other hand, it has been argued (Anderson 2010b) that the final piece of the...

When more than one author has the same surname and the same year

It is unlikely that this will happen. If it does, you can avoid confusion by including the authors' initials, too.

It is clear that the factory was in a bad state of repair (Smith, K., 2002).

However, some writers have argued (Smith, P., 2002) that more government funding...

Direct quotations

When you quote directly (using the author's own words), you should put these in quotation marks, as well as giving the author's name, date and page number(s) from where the quotation was taken (in brackets). Use the abbreviations 'p.' and 'pp.' for page and pages.

"The Eastern question gained particular agency in the wake of the French Revolution, a revolution that frightened all the royal families of Europe, since its ideas denied the legitimacy of them all. The monarchies decided therefore to crush the revolutionaries." (Ansary, 2009, p.241).

If the original document has no page numbers

Websites for example do not usually have page numbers. Therefore, just do the same as for a normal non-electronic quotation, minus a page number.

If you want to miss out part of the original quotation

A series of dots (usually three) indicates that a part of the original quotation has been missed out. You should also do this if you open a quotation part way through a sentence.

"The Eastern question gained particular agency in the wake of the French Revolution, a revolution that frightened all the royal families of Europe...The monarchies decided therefore to crush the revolutionaries." (Ansary, 2009, p.241).

If you want to add words to make a quotation clearer

If you decide to do this, you need to put your own extra words in square brackets.

"They [the European monarchies] assumed this would be easy since the revolution had thrown France into such turmoil," (Ansary, 2009, p.241)

Secondary referencing (when a source is cited within another source)

It is okay to cite a piece of work mentioned or quoted within another author's work. This is known as a secondary reference. In the text of your assignment, you must cite both the original source and the secondary source – where you actually read it – using the words 'quoted in' for a direct quotation or 'cited in' for a summary of the original.

Pearson (2002, cited in Kreefeld, 2004) puts forward the argument that survey was flawed because...

Creating a list of references or bibliography

The list of references or bibliography (or both) comes at the end of your assignment. The purpose of the list of references or bibliography is to show the sources you have used when writing your assignment and to give the reader enough information to find these if required. For these reasons, the list must be clear, consistent and full.

The difference between a list of references and a bibliography is as follows: a list of references includes only sources cited in the text of your assignment, whereas a bibliography includes further reading relevant to the text. Consult your course notes or ask your teacher which you should include.

The list of references or bibliography is always organised alphabetically according to authors' names (or the name of an organisation or company if no author name is available).

How to reference: books

Take the information from the title page of the book and not the front cover. Include the following information in the correct order.

- Author(s), editor(s) or, if not available, the organisation which produced the book
- Year of publication (in brackets)
- Title and subtitle (if any) – <u>underlined</u>, or **bold**, or in *italics* and followed by a full stop. Be consistent in your choice
- Series and individual number (if any), followed by a full stop
- Edition if not the first – for example, '2nd ed.'
- Place of publication if known, followed by a comma
- Name of publisher, followed by a full stop

Barmby, N. (2006) **The end of the British adventure in the East**. 4th ed. London, Macmillan.

How to reference: electronic books

Often you may read a book which is available online. This is different from referencing a website (see below). If the web address is very long, just include enough of it to identify the site from where the book came.

- Author(s), editor(s) or, if not available, the organisation which produced the book
- Print version year, or the electronic version year if no print version is available (in brackets)
- Title and subtitle (if any) – underlined, or **bold**, or in *italics* and followed by a full stop
- The word 'Internet' in [square brackets] followed by a comma
- Print version place of publication, followed by a comma
- Print version publisher, followed by a full stop
- The words 'Available from', followed by a colon

- The internet location from where the book was accessed

- The internet address, in <angled brackets>

- The word 'Accessed' and the date you viewed the book in [square brackets], followed by a full stop

Dillon, S. (2011) My favourite love poems [Internet], Oxford, Oxford University Press. Available from: Netlibrary <http://www.netLibrary.com> [Accessed 29 May 2012].

How to reference: a chapter in an edited collection of writings

It is important to include the name of the editor of a book in the bibliography as this is the information required to trace it in a library catalogue.

- Author of chapter or section

- Year of publication (in brackets)

- Title of chapter or section, followed by a full stop

- The word 'In,' followed by a colon

- The author or editor of the book or collected work (abbreviate 'editor' to 'ed.')

- Title and subtitle (if any) – <u>underlined</u>, or **bold**, or in *italics* and followed by a full stop

- Place of publication, followed by a comma

- Name of publisher, followed by a full stop

- The page numbers of the section referred to, followed by a full stop

Wahlih, K. (2002) Realism or naturalism? In: Neehan, G. ed. **European art of the nineteenth century**. London, Fulmer Press, pp.34-52.

How to reference: journal articles

- Author of the article

- Year of publication (in brackets)

- Title of the article, followed by a full stop

- Title of the journal – <u>underlined</u>, or **bold**, or in *italics* and followed by a comma

- Volume

- Issue or part number (in brackets), and month or season of the year, followed by a comma

- Page numbers of the article, followed by a full stop

Delaware, H. (2012) The role of gender in higher education. **Journal of education**, 5 (VI) May, pp.234-246.

How to reference: newspaper articles

- Author of the article; if no name is given use the title

- Year of publication (in brackets)

- Title of the article, followed by a full stop

- Title of the newspaper – <u>underlined</u>, or **bold**, or in *italics* and followed by a comma

- Date (no year needed), followed by a comma

- Page number(s) of article, followed by a full stop

O'Leary, S. (2006) The easiest way to get thin and fit. **The Guardian,** 29 May, p.7.

How to reference: electronic journal articles

If the web address is very long, just include enough of it to identify the site from where the journal came.

- Author or editor
- Year (in brackets)
- Title of article, followed by a full stop
- Title of journal, <u>underlined</u>, or **bold**, or in *italics*
- The word 'Internet' in [square brackets] followed by a comma
- Volume number
- Issue or part number (in brackets), and month or season of the year, followed by a comma

- Page numbers, followed by a full stop

- The words 'Available from', followed by a colon

- The internet address, in <angled brackets>

- The word 'Accessed' and the date you viewed the article in [square brackets], followed by a full stop

Leeman, G. (2000) How to remain clear of debt. **Financial gazette** [Internet], 35 (5) November. Available from: <http://www.fianancialgazette.com> [Accessed 21 November 2002]

How to reference: electronic newspaper articles

- Author or editor

- Year (in brackets)

- Title of article, followed by a full stop

- Title of journal, underlined, or **bold**, or in *italics*

- The word 'Internet' in [square brackets] followed by a comma

- Date (no year needed), followed by a comma, then page numbers or online equivalent, followed by a full stop

- The words 'Available from', followed by a colon

- The internet address, in <angled brackets>

- The word 'Accessed' and the date you viewed the article in [square brackets], followed by a full stop

Killybeg, H. (2009) The end of the golden era. **The Times** [Internet], 16 June. Available from: <http://www.thetimes.co.uk/business> [Accessed 17 July 2010]

How to reference: web pages

Because internet pages may only be available for a short time, keep a personal copy as evidence that the information existed.

- Author or editor

- Year (in brackets). If no year is available, use 'n.d.'

- Title, underlined, or **bold**, or in *italics*

- The word 'Internet' in [square brackets] followed by a comma

- Edition if available, followed by a full stop

- Place of publication, followed by a comma

- Publisher if known, followed by a full stop

- The words 'Available from', followed by a colon

- The internet address, in <angled brackets>

- The word 'Accessed' and the date you viewed the page in [square brackets], followed by a full stop

BBC (2012) **London to host electric car race in 2014** [Internet], London, BBC. Available from: <http://www.bbc.co.uk/news/uk-england-london-21725324> [Accessed 10 June 2012]

How to reference: theses and dissertations

Include the name of the awarding body, for example, University

Kurdistan-Hewler. Apart from that, the content and order is the same

as for a book.

Falmouth, H. (1996) **The reception of early Italian art in Germany, 1810-**

1850. Ph.D. thesis, University of St. Andrews

How to reference: encyclopaedia entries

- Author or editor

- Year of publication (in brackets)

- Title of article, followed by a comma

- The word 'in'

- Title of encyclopaedia, underlined, or **bold**, or in *italics*

- Volume number if available, followed by a comma

- Edition number, followed by a full stop

- Place of publication, followed by a comma

- Publisher, followed by a full stop

- Page number(s) of definition, followed by a full stop

Heep, H. (1996) Market gardens, in: **New Encyclopaedia Britannica**, vol. 17, 8th revised edition. London, Encyclopaedia Britannica.

How to reference: dictionary entries

Because dictionaries do not normally have an author, the reference is based on the title of the work.

- Title of dictionary, <u>underlined</u>, or **bold**, or in *italics*

- Year of publication (in brackets)

- Volume number if necessary, followed by a comma

- Edition number, followed by a full stop

- Place of publication, followed by a comma

- Publisher, followed by a comma

- Page number(s) of definition, followed by a full stop

Oxford English dictionary. (2002) vol. 7, 2nd ed. Oxford, Clarendon, p.167.

How to reference: online images

Images should always be referenced, even if they are available for free. Some websites request that you cite extra information before you are allowed to use the image.

- Title of image, or a description, <u>underlined</u>, or **bold**, or in *italics*
- Year (in brackets)
- The words 'Online image' or 'Online video' in [square brackets], followed by a full stop
- The words 'Available from', followed by a colon
- The internet address, in <angled brackets>
- The word 'Accessed' and the date you viewed the image in [square brackets], followed by a full stop

Image of effects of global warning. (2010) [Online image]. Available from:

<http://www.imageprovider.org> [Accessed 22 June 2012]

How to reference: original works of art

- Artist

- Year the work was produced (in brackets)

- Title of work, <u>underlined</u>, or **bold**, or in *italics*

- Material type in [square brackets], followed by a full stop

- The words 'held at'

- The location of the gallery or museum, followed by a full stop

Ruysch, R. (1685) **Flowers in a vase** [oil on canvas]. Held at The National

Gallery, London

www.ingramcontent.com/pod-product-compliance
Lightning Source LLC
Chambersburg PA
CBHW060343290526
45791CB00004B/1514